In the Dark:

Tales from Narcissistic Abuse Survivors

By Tenishia Danielle

Copyright © 2023 by Empower Your Empire LLC

ISBN 979-8-9853302-4-3 (Paperback)

Please visit our website at www.tenishiawrites.com for more books

If you would like to contact Tenishia Danielle for speaking opportunities email her at:

TenishiaWrites@gmail.com

Note from Author

First of all I would like to thank everyone for taking the time to purchase and read this book. This book is intended to help people that may be in a narcissistic relationship find the strength they need to remove themselves from it. I also want to help those that have survived those relationships find a healing place through shared experiences and start to put themselves first.

The contents of this book may be hard to get through if you have experienced similar situations so I encourage you to read at your own pace and know that you are not alone. This is the first of many books on this subject it is my hope that by sharing these stories that more people will speak up on their experiences and share them with me to write about. If you want to share your story for the next book please email me at TenishiaWrites@gmail.com.

The First Step

"If everyone could come to have a seat so we can get started," Margaret said. Before each of you get started and ready to share your story with us I want to thank you all for your willingness to share the hurt, trauma, and feelings that you had to go through in your relationship with a narcissist in your life. I know this is not gonna be easy but I know that sharing your story is going to help someone else. One thing I want you guys to know is that narcissists do not pick weak people so the fact that you had to endure them just means that you were a strong supply for them and the evidence that you are still here is proof.

Where are my manners allow me to introduce myself my name is Margaret and I have been free of my narcissistic relationship for 10 years now. I started this narcissistic abuse survivor's group 7 years ago as a way to help me heal from the abuse I endured. Because the type of abuse, we go through a lot of times leaves no physical scars our family and mutual friends do not believe and cannot empathize with the trauma that we all know is real. My ex-husband left me after draining me mentally, emotionally, spiritually, and financially. He turned his back on our children when he could no longer control them and moved on to take care of a whole new family.

When he left us I was at rock bottom and when he married the woman he cheated on me for years with after only 3 months after the divorce I felt like I was spiraling out of control. I started talking to a therapist but by the third one, it became clear I needed to speak with someone who went through what I went through to start the healing process. I started searching for groups but at that time there were no narcissistic abuse survivor groups near me so I started my own. In the first session, I shared my story with a group of ten people and the reaction of understanding and empathy had my emotions on high. In the years I spent in that abusive relationship my tears were always ignored, ridiculed, and silenced after a while so I suffered alone. But not that day I was met with similar stories that made it seem as though they had lived with the same person that I did all those years.

I hope that as each of you shares your story with us you can have the same healing experience we had in those weeks that followed. Today we will be hearing from five individuals as they share their experiences with the narcissist that was in their life. Please give them your undivided attention and your unwavering support as they courageously tell us about their journey through hell.

Mommy Dearest

Hi everyone my name is Sherelle and I am a survivor of a narcissistic mother. Your mother is the first person that is supposed to love, nurture, and care for you unfortunately I did not have that experience. My earliest memory of my mother Mary was of her and my father fighting and her throwing a vase that missed me by an inch, I was five.

My mother Mary was said to be the spoiled youngest of her siblings but as my mom, it was beyond spoiled. If I had to sum up my relationship with her it would be cold, brash, and heartless. My mother only cared about herself and her instant gratification. As I was growing up I often wondered why she even had me and my four siblings but the older I got it became clear we were just pawns she used to get sympathy as a single parent. She looked for any way she could to benefit from being left by her husband to raise kids alone.

My mother was a gambler and loved to party as a child I would watch her get ready to leave us numerous times to go out all night to be free. In my adolescent years, I became the parent to my siblings who did not listen, and the maid and cook to my family who lived like animals. My mother provided no structure but ruled with an iron fist and ruled that you "do as I say not as I do." My voice was silenced early on and I was conditioned to comply with her or be subjected to her tantrums and punishment.

I was a straight-A student throughout school hoping one day I would hear "I'm proud of you Sherelle!" But that day never came so by the time I was a junior in high school I decided to do what I wanted since the praise was never going to come. To this day I cannot tell you anything she taught me about womanhood, motherhood, or even humanity that helped me in life.

Every holiday I spent in her home was about her and Christmas was the worst. My siblings and I would spend the whole Christmas season anticipating gifts that never came not even a tree made it to our home. On Christmas mornings we would be in tears coming down the stairs to nothing and asking her why. I can still hear her say, "You better be glad you are in the land of the living that's your gift!" She would then make us go make her breakfast and bring it to her in bed like she was the Queen of Sheba.

I started working at 14 as a maid in a hotel. My mother made sure that as soon as I got paid all of my money would be gone. I was told to go grocery shopping, give her money for bills, loan her money that was never going to be repaid, and was left with just enough money to get me back and forth to work until I got paid again. I was working to have clothes for school but after all of the expenses she came up with I could only afford clothes from the consignment store which were old clothes and fatigue. Mary could care less of the embarrassment I had going to school in hand-me-downs after working all summer.

Before I turned 16 my mother decided to ground me for a year and I have no idea why. She was not the one that felt she needed to explain herself or apologize for anything. My younger sister and I were both punished and made to stay home. At the end of August while home, my mother started screaming in excruciating pain. In a panic, I called my aunt to come to our home because I honestly thought my mother was dying. She was complaining of pain in her stomach but the screams and crying is all I saw and that was the only time I ever remember her showing another emotion outside of anger and frustration toward me. She looked helpless and I almost felt compassion toward her vulnerability and her what seemed like a genuine need for my help. That was short-lived because after my aunt took her to the hospital we got a call that night that our mother had successfully given birth to a baby girl!! She never told us she was pregnant and had now had another child for me to raise. I was mortified at the thought that not only did she hide the pregnancy from us she put us through all types of hell with her mood swings and unreasonable punishments all because she was pregnant. To top it off when she was going into labor and we all thought she was dying she never let on the reason for her pain and let us believe she was not coming back alive. What kind of person let alone a mother does that to their children?!?!

When I turned 16 I begged her for a party and she relented but only if she and her friends were there. I wish I never asked! While my friends and I were in the living room they spent the evening laughing at us and berating everything from our looks to the clothes we had on I was so embarrassed. But of course, I could not let her know that and had to show her appreciation for even letting me have a birthday party which was the only one I ever had.

My father left when I was five after their years of fighting over who would stay home and parent the kids they had since she was not willing to stay home and he wasn't either he left. Shortly after I turned 16 he showed up at our house trying to start a relationship with us. Well if it is serving Ms. Mary then no one can benefit. She started an argument with him and he cut off all communication with us. I was crushed I felt like he was my only hope to escape her and now he was gone, again.

After that I started plotting my escape I decided to move across the country to stay with my cousin. When I told her my plan to leave I thought some part of her would want me to stay but I was gifted a suitcase instead. A year later I left the state and left her to care for my youngest siblings and she was upset she could no longer use me. She started her smear campaign against my siblings telling them I left them not her and that I did not love them and only she loved them. Even though I was the one that decided to leave she made sure I knew I was discarded from all of their lives unless I was going to come back to be under her control again. That day never came and her lies caused my siblings to hate me and we never repaired our relationship even when she died.

My life after leaving her was not easy but I felt free. I became a mother and decided to be the opposite of my own. I made a point to communicate with my children, build them up and encourage them. I have been in other narcissistic relationships with friends, romantic partners, and other family members but none like the one with my mother Mary. Her callous behavior ensured that our house was never home and that survival not love was the foundation I was raised in. My grandmother was the one who showed me how to love and I am thankful for the lessons I learned from her about being selfless, nurturing, and kind.

Although Mary never taught me anything her lack of support, attention, and love caused me to become the person I am today. I made it my mission to never make my kids or any human feel the way I felt the first part of my life. I celebrate and love my children and now grandchildren even though I did not have the example growing up. The fantasies that I had of how my life would be if I was ever able to break free from Mary's rule I made come true.

It wasn't until recently that I even found out there was a name from who my mother was to me and that it was an actual personality disorder. Although it does not excuse the trauma she put me through I am finding peace knowing I did not break under her rule and that today I am not broken.

Thank you so much for sharing with us Sherelle! said, Margaret. I could not imagine having to go through that with my mother. There have been numerous studies on the making of a narcissist and after what you went through to be able to still feel and be a compassionate person without becoming what you were raised by is remarkable. The trauma that we endure as children oftentimes shape us to become a narcissist or an empath. The silent encoding that is done to us through that trauma creates a response to either make everyone pay for what we went through or make sure that no one has to experience it from us setting us apart from that trauma. The damage that a narcissist does is meant to annihilate who you are at the core to drain the strong supply that you are until death or you decide to discard them first.

Our next story comes from Alexis this is extremely hard for her to share since her relationship did end in death. Please give her support as she shares her story.

Til Death Did We Part

Hi everyone as Margaret mentioned my name is Alexis. I am going to try my best to get through this without crying but I am still raw so please bare with me. Growing up the middle sibling and only girl in my family of 10 I had to be tough. I grew up in the Jim Crow era in the south and went to an integrated school where from day one I was hated just for what I looked like which made me stay on the defense. Even though I had to pretend to be tough to avoid fighting I lived my childhood in fear and insecurity. My brother's teasing me for being the oddball in the home and being the oddball outside of the home always made me feel so alone like no one ever understood me.

My father was in the military so being adaptable to my ever-changing environment at a young age caused me to build a wall of protection around my mind and heart early on. My relationship with my mother was strained but I admired her and wanted to be like her to feel some type of connection with anyone. At a young age a few of my siblings and I were sent away to live with distant relatives for a few years in the big city. I saw everything from drugs to prostitution my young eyes widened with adult things I would never forget. While being in that home that sense of loneliness found new emotions anger and resentment. How could my parents just give us up without knowing if we were in a safe place? Why would my mom not want to keep me her only girl who wanted to be like her? I was so upset with them but my anger was mostly with her.

We returned home after a couple of years and gone was that timid girl who was afraid to fight. I was so angry that the slightest mean look in my direction erupted into the beast I felt was inside and it no longer mattered if they were black or white. I spent my teen years fighting and by the time I was a senior I decided to follow in my father's footsteps and join the military.

At 18 I started boot camp for the Army and fought alongside men and women for my country. The more I tried to be tough the more that little girl who wanted acceptance from both parents showed up in my relationships. The abuse and cheating I endured trying to be loved by the men in my life caused that wall to go back up and taller than ever.

After many failed relationships I decided to stop trying and focus on my career in the military. Five years shy of my retirement I was stationed in Germany and that's where I met Terry. When I saw him standing there in his uniform I was in awe he had to be at least six foot six bald with the biggest arms I had ever seen. Imagine a black Hulk and you would have Terry. He approached me with a big smile and I felt that wall starting to crumble. It must've been his size making me feel safe but I found myself mesmerized. He asked me out to a restaurant on base and I quickly said yes.

On our first date, I almost canceled it because he was almost an hour late. He called and said he had a bad reaction to shellfish and had to wait for his allergy medicine to kick in but to please wait for him. I instantly felt bad for the thoughts of canceling on him and never seeing him again. When he finally arrived I thought it was weird that he did not seem to have any signs of an allergic reaction but quickly dismissed it since I kind of still felt bad. While on the date he listened intently to my life story as I felt so comfortable telling him all of the things I went through in my childhood, my insecurities, and how the men in my life had treated me. In hindsight, I realize I was giving him all the ammunition to use against me but at that moment I thought his intent to get to know me better was so attractive. He mirrored all of my trauma it was almost like we grew up in the same traumatic home filled with abandonment and mistreatment.

Terry told me his ex-wife was terrible to him a cheater who always lied. He said he was so hurt that no one ever treated him right and he prayed every night to find someone like me. I was floored it was at that moment I felt he was the one God had for me. I had never even heard of the term "love bombing" but over the next few weeks that is exactly what happened to me. We went on date after date and spoke on the phone for hours while he asked me everything under the sun about me weird questions like what is my biggest fear, what a man needs to do to show you, love, do you believe in divorce. In the conversations, I answered without ever asking why because his interest was so intense I thought he just was trying to get to know me.

In the first 3 months, we moved so fast and he proposed before I even met anyone in his family. He convinced me they were terrible people who he hadn't spoken to in years and he wanted to focus on me and our future. We both only had a few years left to retire so we frequently discussed our lives after retirement. He had big plans of starting his gym because he loved working out and helping people change their bodies through nutrition.

I was supportive of his dreams and shortly after we got married at the courthouse he started working for a local gym as a trainer. Once he started working there he started taking on the clients that he worked with outside of the gym hours to do cardio outdoors. I started to notice he was working later and later and I asked him if he was sure all he was doing was working since we did not share bank accounts I never saw any difference in the money coming into the home.

He completely blew up on me calling me insecure and using all of the information I gave him about my insecurities against me. I cried so hard that night I almost had an anxiety attack. How could the person I love so much talk to me like that and with such disgust and anger? I never got an answer to my question but what I did get is the first taste of the real Terry.

Over the next 10 years, I felt like I was living in a mirror maze. Everyone loved Terry he was so charismatic and charming to everyone except me. My family and friends loved how funny he was and he was so helpful to them. He would joke about me in front of them but because he was saying it in a joking manner I had to play it off in front of them otherwise he would gaslight me into going off on him making me look crazy. As much as my family and friends loved him he talked about them so badly behind their backs. I was living with the real-life Dr. Jekyll and Mr. Hyde I got the monster behind the mask his mental and emotional abuse was so bad my body started breaking out into hives from the stress he put me through.

One day he started sleeping in the guest room and that is when I started being tormented at night. It was almost like there was a spirit in my room that was beating me up at night. I started losing my hair and was so sleep-deprived I felt like I was going insane. When I would ask him why he would not sleep with me he would blow me off saying he was working on paperwork all night and did not want to keep me up. I told him how I was having trouble sleeping and he looked me so coldly in the eye and said "maybe you are going crazy" I felt a chill in my spine and walked away absolutely devastated. I wanted so badly to have the version of Terry I fell in love with but this monster was a shell of who I thought I knew.

Just when I thought I was going to die or go completely insane I had a conversation with a friend who recommended that I pray that whatever is tormenting me at night be sent back to the sender. I took it a step further and had a spiritual advisor come to my house while Terry was at work to pray over my room and they told me they did feel that spirit and prayed and open the windows to let it out. Over the next few weeks, I began to get more rest and started to feel like my old self again. I started working out, eating better, and feeling stronger each day.

One day Terry came home from work or so I thought but when I looked him in the eyes I could tell he had been crying. I asked him what was wrong and he collapsed into my arms sobbing saying he did not have much time left. Time left for what? I asked completely confused in between sobs he said… to live. "What?!?!" I screamed leaning back to look him in the eyes. He then told me he just left the doctor and they told him he has stage 4 cancer and he only has a few months left to live. I was shocked and felt my world crumbling. He explained he found out a couple of months ago but thought he could beat it but now knows that was not going to happen.

I think I felt all the emotions well up in me at that moment trying to process what he was telling me. Not only did he hide his diagnosis and pretend as if nothing had happened he is dying when just a couple of months ago I felt like I was. I couldn't process it fast enough and went into autopilot there's gotta be another doctor that can change this I have to pray I can't lose him like this. Even after all the pain he put me through my mind would not let me think of life without him.

I went to his next appointment with him and the doctor explained what he already told me there was nothing they could do but try to make him as comfortable as possible. When the doctor stepped out Terry told me to sit down and that he wanted to tell me something. "I've been praying on this and I feel like it best to tell you the truth. You know all those late nights where I said I was working?" He said. "Yes," I said confused as to where he was going with this. "I have been having an affair with one of my clients for the last 5 years I am so sorry," he said his eyes welling up with tears. I was too stunned to speak so he kept going. "I know I made you feel like you were wrong for thinking I was cheating on you and made you feel like you were crazy but now that I am no longer going to be here I need to leave with a clean slate. I am so messed up inside no one ever made me feel like I was worth anything and I think I just wasn't used to someone caring for me as you did so I stepped out on you. Now I know this is a lot but there's more. I have a 3-

year-old and his name is Terry jr. I know I never helped you with the household bills but it's because she needed my help and I had to take care of my son. I knew you had the money to pay for everything so I did not think you needed me which is why I found someone who did. I wish you were enough but the truth is you weren't Alexis I do need you now and I am so sorry I know you are a godly one who forgives so I am begging you to find it in your heart to forgive me." He said now sitting on the bed with his head down and shoulders sunken.

I felt like I was going to pass out like a ton of bricks hit me at once. This had to be a dream some type of nightmare this cannot be the man that I loved the one I gave everything in me to. But as I blinked and looked at him sitting there I am not going to lie I felt like I was going to be on the next episode of snapped. I walked away from him and was in a daze as I walked down the hospital hallway should I go to my car or floor 7 to check myself into the psych ward? All those years I knew what I felt was right and he gaslit me called me insecure and every name under the sun and I was right!! I cannot believe he is choosing now to tell me this knowing he is dying and needs me to take care of him. I am going to tell him to call that bitch he was sleeping with and oh my God a son!? He told me he was ok with us not having kids and that I was all he wanted and needed in his life this cannot be real. I somehow made it to my car and I sat there and cried and screamed until I was shaking. "How could he do this to me after all I did for him? He can go to hell after all he put me through fuck him!"

I drove home and when I got there he was in the driveway just standing there looking at me with tear-soaked eyes. Run him over Alexis! I heard a voice in my head say but as I was going to put my foot on the gas he dropped to his knees and started begging me to help him. I felt my heart soften as I found myself seeing the Terry I fell in love with. He looked so helpless and I couldn't help but feel sorry for him. I parked the truck and walked up to him and said "Only because I am choosing to honor God and our vows I will forgive you." He slowly stood up and hugged me and thanked me for being such a godly woman.

The next 2 weeks I felt like I had the Terry back that I fell in love with he was so nice to me that I felt that wall coming down that I had built back up after years of his torment. He let me know that he had made sure to have the house paid off when he did pass away and that I would not have to worry about his funeral arrangements as they had been paid for as well. He was even polite thanking me for helping him after his treatments which he had stopped even saying excuse me years ago. I was in bliss for 2 weeks…. Until his treatment stopped working that's when the mask came off again. After that nothing I did was right his food was nasty his bed was too hard his water too cold. He began sneaking to make late-night phone calls and he became his old self again. He was losing weight rapidly and he wasn't as scary as the Hulk he used to be so I found myself giving him back everything he gave to me no more silence and taking it he was going to hear me and hear me.

Just as the doctor said his time had come and on the day he was supposed to go to hospice he died. I had just left to get some of his clothes and received a call from the doctor he had just passed away. I felt numb even though I knew the time was close I still did not want to believe it. I should have felt free but instead, I felt devastated I gave this man everything and left nothing for myself. How can I come back from this?

As I was cleaning out his things and preparing for his funeral I found the paperwork that he signed to pay off our home and the date he signed it was so familiar. I looked at my phone calendar and it was so odd that was the same day I started being tormented in my sleep. That's weird I thought but kept going through his things as I was going through his office I opened his bottom cabinet and this book fell out. I picked it up and was shocked it was a hoodoo book on how to cast spells. He had a page bookmarked and I opened it and my eyes instantly welled up in tears the page was instructions on how to invoke spirits to torment and kill someone. Terry was not preparing for his death he was preparing for mines! When I had that spiritual advisor come to get rid of the spirit and return it to the sender HE WAS THE SENDER! In his attempt to kill me, it was reversed and killed him. Again I was devastated I love and hated this man even in death he had a hold on me. I want so badly to just hate him but I find myself still grieving the loss of his presence in my life even if those good times were short I still miss them and who I believed he was. I am so hurt and angry about the time I spent loving someone who never loved me. I hope one day not to feel like this and I know sharing today is a step in the right direction but I do not want to feel this way I want to heal.

Alexis I know that took a lot for you to tell us your story and I appreciate you for standing up for yourself and sharing it. Narcissists count on us to stay silent while they torture us and can make us feel wrong for telling the truth. Even though Terry is no longer alive by you speaking it out loud I hope you can free yourself from the burden of countless times you felt you did not have a voice. You mentioned in your story that he brought up your faith to manipulate you into forgiving him. Narcissists tend to use God to benefit them and guilt trip their victims into compliance.

Throughout history and all over the world the evilest leaders used their narcissistic personalities to bring the nations they ruled to their knees and under their control. Hitler, Stalin, and even Putin have all shown their narcissistic behaviors for the world to see and caused many lives to no longer exist by abusing the nations they were supposed to lead and protect. Narcissists do not care who they use to maintain their control even kids are often used in their scheme to maintain control.

Another ploy that narcissists use to maintain control over their victims is to isolate them from anyone they feel they cannot control. You will find yourself losing touch with friends and family to avoid conflict with the narcissist who without reason or explanation does not like them. The sacrifices and allowances you make just to keep the peace in your life eventually will leave you no longer able to recognize the person you are within that relationship. Next, we will be hearing from Trevor who was in a 25-year relationship and marriage with his narcissistic ex-wife. Please show him your support by giving him your attention.

Surviving Charli

Thank you, Ms. Margaret, what's up everybody I am Trevor but I go by Big Trev. I am from Cali and in my hood, we stand on respect and loyalty. My dad was the king in my family even though he died when I was only 5 his legacy was all everyone ever talked about. He knew how to make money and put my whole family on. Growing up I was young, wild, and reckless I stayed in fights, and winning all of them wasn't even a question everyone knew stepping to Big Trev meant taking an L.

I stayed in the streets making money and because I was always tall and handsome, grown women used to flirt with me and named me "grown man" so they wouldn't feel guilty stepping to a boy. My mama and grandma tried their best to raise me but without a man around I made up my manhood code as I went and it was ingrained in me that no other man was above me in any hood or room. I took pride in my manhood and when I was just a kid I became an uncle to my nephew and became his mentor and male figure. I made sure to school him how to carry himself so no one would test him.

Being the protector came easy to me and I took pride in being the provider for the family by any means necessary. I was raised during the height of the crack epidemic and both my mom and her husband were addicts so making money to stay off the streets was my priority. I went to school but after getting into yet another fight and beating that fool down the school expelled me. As the saying goes an idle mind is the devil's playground I had way too much time on my hands which meant trouble always found me.

My homies started linking with these females from
Berkeley and told me they had one they thought I would
like. Right before they made the introduction they tried
to warn me they think she is a little crazy so be careful
with her. I blew it off because in my mind there is no one
out here male or female that can run me and if she cute
she gotta get down with my program not the other way
around you feel me? Looking back now I should've
listened but hindsight is always 20/20 you know?
Anyways they introduced us her name was Charlotte
but she went by Charli.

Charli grew up in a good neighborhood with money but
she somehow always came to my hood to be in my
room even when she was supposed to be in school.
Because she already had more credits than she needed
for school she would sneak off to my crib and all we did
was smash. I don't think we went on one date in the first
months of being together so even though it shouldn't
have been too much of a surprise she wound up
pregnant. At that time I was only 17 and she was 16 so
we both were scared but me I knew I had to step up and
take care of my responsibilities. Her mom was super
strict and a bible toting Christian so she was too scared
to tell her so we hid the pregnancy for the first 6 months
trying to figure out what to do. Now because I was
raised by women I know when they are pregnant they
go through bad mood swings but Charli's seemed
different. It was like dealing with the exorcist if she did
not get what she wanted when she wanted it. I ain't
gonna lie I felt guilty as hell for getting her pregnant and
she wouldn't let me forget that I ruined all her plans to
go to the top HBCU in the country. Now we all know it

takes two to get down and I ain't never had to force no female to get with me but I let her have it since she was carrying a piece of me it wasn't worth the energy you feel me?

One of her homegirls was also pregnant and it got back to her moms that Charli was too and that's when all hell broke loose. Her moms came to my house talking down to me and my mama saying I wasn't raised right and how ghetto we were. I felt like I was about to flash on this female she had the wrong one and in the wrong hood but again I know my part in it so I told myself to stay respectful even though I wasn't getting it from her. She tried to get Charli to get rid of our baby and I was devastated I had already started planning for fatherhood coming up with names and even buying clothes and this lady was about to end all of that. Because she was so far along it was too late and she had to have our baby.

When our little girl was born I knew my life had to change and I was willing to do whatever it took so I gave up my old life to ensure I would stay in our child's life. All the homies I used to run with, the hustling everything was over the moment I knew I was having her and I never looked back to that life. I guess you could say having her saved my life because up until that point, my life was leading to prison or the graveyard. I told Charli how important being an active father in our child's life was to me and I was going make sure she got everything she wanted in life for giving me the chance to be a dad. Even though I did not know her that well I was committed to staying with her if it meant staying in my kid's life.

I wanted to be the best dad I could be even though I did not have an example growing up my goal was to always provide and protect them at all costs. When Charli saw how much it meant to me that was exactly what she used to torment me. I remember when our baby girl was 3 months old Charli started going out with her cousins and siblings almost every night leaving me at home to watch the baby. At first I didn't mind since I had already given up my old life being a parent was my focus. But I started to notice when we did go out she was little too flirty with dudes in front of me and they felt real comfortable being on her so I had to check them. She would always make it seem like I was overreacting but after seeing that I didn't really trust her but if that's how she was going to get down I would just focus on my kid.

Every time she would hang out with her family she would come home and start arguing with me about what we didn't have and how she is not used to struggling. I would listen to her talk about what she wanted to do in her life and me wanting to be the provider started coming up with a plan to make it happen. She was materialistic wanting to have the latest and greatest of everything she saw someone else have which I never understood. One day one of her friends told her about her new hustle in doing fashion shows and all the celebrities she meets doing it. Well that was music to Charli's ears she already thought she was a star and to have the chance to be in the room with celebrities and make money she was all in. She came home and started telling me this is what she wanted to focus on and that she would start making clothes right away. Since I was the one making the money I started using my extra income to buy her fabrics and help her get events set up. The more I did to make her dream happen the more she made feel like I wasn't good enough to be standing beside her. I was so focused on making sure the behind the scenes went well I never noticed how our new life had changed a small demon into a huge monster. She went into full diva mode demanding more otherwise I would have to hear her tantrums and get guilt tripped into making her life better since she was a teen mom and missed out on the life she felt she deserved.

We kept having kids and before I knew it we were on kid number four. By that time we were full time entrepreneurs in the fashion industry making millions. Whenever we had events at clubs or out of town Charli made sure to go without me leaving me home to take care of the kids. She was living her dream as the face of the company mingling with celebrities and traveling the world doing fashion shows. Our only conversations surrounded around how to make more money that she was spending as fast as we were getting it. Looking back I think I was depressed and my only friend became food. I blew up to over 500 lbs and could barely fit into my now 7x clothes. I felt like I was being swallowed alive by fat but as long as I had my kids and could stay in their lives I went with her program.

I started noticing she would pick a fight at the same time every week and leave the house for hours and come back like nothing happened. In the back of my mind I started thinking she was seeing someone else but I was so detached part of me did not care as long as no drama was in my life. She always thought she was better than my family since hers had a little bit of money so anytime I wanted to spend time with my family or even bring my kids around them she would have a melt down or start a huge argument with me over it. I do not argue so slowly I stopped being around my family or if I did it would be a short period time which just made my depression worse. The bigger I got the more she would talk about me making jokes about my weight, my snoring or just anything to be mean. Now mind you she was never a beauty queen and was big too but I never cut her down that's not my get down you feel me?

She always had her family around her either living with us or off of us and anytime she had an issue with me she would go straight to them or social media with it but not to me. I would find myself getting phone calls from family members asking me if everything was ok and I would be so confused but they would let me know of a post she made about me and issues I had no idea we were having. She always wanted the attention and sympathy but never gave it to anyone else. If I would try to give her feedback on her designs or how things could be better she would get in her feelings and try to say something to cut me down. For someone that was so cold and heartless she could never take what she dished out.

When our oldest daughter was graduating from high school my aunt and grandma decided to come to the graduation which meant staying with us for a few days. You would have thought they were moving in without her knowing she talked about them so bad and started yelling asking when they would be leaving it was so bad my aunt said she would never step foot in our home again. She loved hearing that and her mom was at the house for longer but because she hated my family too they both could careless my family wasn't coming around.

My favorite cousin died and I was so crushed not only did she not come to the funeral with me she acted as if it was just another day. I took my son with me to the funeral and we stayed for a little over a week to help with funeral arrangements and the actual funeral. Charli kept calling and harassing me telling me I better get back home and went even further and shut off my debit card so I could no longer help with my cousin's funeral. When I finally got back home and saw her it was like looking the devil in the eyes she had no soul. Anyone that can do that when someone dies cannot be human.

Even after the incident with my aunt and grandma my mother who I hadn't seen in years because of Charli came to see me for a few days with my sister. As soon as Charli heard she was coming she left town with my oldest daughter and stayed gone the entire time. I was so happy to see my mom being a mama's boy it meant the world to me to have her not just stay with me but to see my life now that I was making money legally and not in any trouble like I was as a teen. Since I wanted to keep the peace I told my mom we were taking the kids on a trip the next day so that Charli would not come home and see her there and cause another scene. That was the last time I saw my mom because shortly after that she went missing.

I was distraught hearing my mother was missing and because of this I could not focus on the business. Instead of Charli understanding she kept trying to get me to stop worrying about my mom and focus on her and making money. I couldn't so she threatened to divorce me if I did not get my act together. I blew her off because I was focused on how to find my mama. One night while we were sitting at the kitchen table we hear a knock at the door I am greeted by a sheriff and served with divorce papers!! I walked back to the table in shock and asked her how could she do this while I was going through this with my mom. She stared blankly and said "I told you I would if you didn't get back to making money for our family!" She then walked away.

A week later my mom was found dead. Charli could careless and I attended the funeral alone. That was the hardest time of my life my only living parent was gone and I had no support. When I got back home Charli being the heartless person she is said she wanted to go to a hookah lounge and that would cheer me up. I don't know if she was high or what but still being devastated I didn't have the energy to argue. When we got there you would think she was celebrating a business win or hangin with a celebrity how happy she was at the lounge. I couldn't take another minute of it and told her I wanted to go home. She then started sobbing right there in the lounge saying she wanted to stay! I looked at her like the crazy person she was embodying and it was in the moment I knew I had to leave her alone.

I did not want a divorce since my life had become just being a father and husband I had nothing left. Our business was slowly dying and I was still mourning the loss of my mom. I told her if she wants this divorce she would have to do it alone. She told me I needed to fight for my family and I looked at her and asked her who am I fighting? You want this divorce go for it. I guess she wanted me to beg her to stay with me but outside of the kids we shared and a business there was nothing connecting us. Once she saw she could no longer control my actions by throwing a tantrum you would think I was public enemy number one she started her plan to destroy me, my character and everything I stood for.

Once we officially separated the more I tried to find myself again outside of the control she tried to have over me the more she plotted to make my life miserable. She started to pull out the ammunition she had built up over the years to control me and my number one weakness was my children. She would use them to manipulate me into doing what she wanted. She deliberately found herself in financial distress because she knew it was in me to make sure my kids were provided for. Every time I tried to build she would do something to make sure I had to focus on her and the kids and have to come back to help them.

The times I would come to the rescue she would treat me like I was the one with the hand out and talk to me so disrespectful and encouraged my kids to do the same. One time I left my place to move in hers to prevent my kids from being evicted before our divorce was finalized and she made sure I knew she moved on by parading her sea of men in my face and staying out all night. It hurt me to see how the relationship I gave most of my life to end like this but the loyalty I had for my family kept me blind to what she had been doing behind my back all of those years.

Even now as much I would like to be a co-parent with her but she is hell bent on making it a nightmare or using me to make the new men in her life jealous by using all the things I did for her against them. I have been spending time self reflecting trying my best to be the best version of myself. I don't regret meeting her because I know without her I would not have my kids but I wish I was not such in a hurry to grow up by sleeping with someone I barely knew. I am finding strength in doing what I love to do instead of what I was made to do and finding myself. I am the co-creator of my life I am committed on making it the best life possible. Being a fighter has always been in me but nothing prepared me for the fight for my life being with her and am so grateful I was able to survive Charli.

Trevor I want to commend you on sharing your story. Men are often silent when it comes to the abuse they go through as if they are not worthy of validation. Narcissistic women count on this and will use your emotions against you so you are conditioned to silence. Rebuilding after being with a narcissist can feel like you are starting at ground zero and most of the time we are after being discarded when they feel they no longer need our supply.

Sharing our stories with the world is the first step in our phoenix rising saga. I know each of you will be greater than you could imagine once you have healed from this trauma. Trevor as much as being a father is the core of who you are I hope you are able to keep being a positive force in your children's lives to combat the narcissist mother they have.

We heard from Trevor and his fight to be a father in a turbulent relationship we will now hear from Charity who survived her narcissistic father. Charity is a ray of light I had the opportunity to mentor and her journey of self love after her narcissistic father died is definitely life changing. Please give her your support and attention.

Nightmare on Elmwood St.

Thank you so much Ms. Margaret I really appreciate your guidance and mentorship. Hey everybody I am Charity like she said. I know there are so many kids that wished they grew up in a two parent home thinking it would be like living with the family of their favorite childhood sitcom. That it would be jokes, love and lessons everyday. My dad Charles had a lot of jokes unfortunately he made the people closest to him the butt of everyone of them. While the world got to see his sense of humor as one of his best qualities we learned to hide the hurt when he got real nasty with his insults disguised as jokes. I can remember as a toddler hearing his big obnoxious laugh and seeing my mom without a smile on her face. Back then I do not remember what he said but I knew I did not like how I felt.

I was an oops baby both my parents were older my dad was 10 years older than my mom when she got pregnant after they had been married only 6 months. They both had abscess teeth and were prescribed penicillin which my mom found out after she was pregnant it cancel out the effects of birth control. My mom's pregnancy was challenging and she picked up a lot of weight which did not go unnoticed by my dad who was big himself but always had something to say about her weight.

My dad was a very dark skinned and my mom was brown skinned so genetically it should not have been a surprise my melanin would be poppin. My dad had 3 sons before his marriage to my mom by a white woman so all his boys were light skinned with wavy and curly hair which he loved to show them off as trophies any chance he got. In public that is, because when we were home they would be on his joking chopping block with the rest of us. My sister who we share the same mom was also lighter skin so he treated her like one of the golden children too.

Before I turned 3 I was light enough to pass his sick paper bag test I guess because up until that point there were many pictures of us and he actually had a smile on his face. When we moved to Elmwood St when I turned 3 all of my color came in at once and I was the spitting image of his sister. Even though I was just a toddler I could feel the distance starting he no longer took pictures with me and all of sudden playing outside for too long became an issue for him.

The older I got the more mean his jokes got and did not stop at just my color he started talking about my weight because I have always been on the thicker than a snicker side. When I started school he started comparing any of my achievements and milestones to my siblings letting me know they were smarter, quicker and more talented than me. Because of the age gap between myself and my siblings I was raised as an only child which just meant the main target for his torment in the home. He became a nightmare that my mom tried her best to protect me from.

Growing up everyone in my family loved music and he was a musician always singing songs that tied to a conversation. I loved to sing and wanted to be in the band my brother's started but that was quickly shut down by him telling me I was not talented enough and they get their talent from him as if we did not share the same DNA. I was crushed and I would find myself trying to learn his favorite songs and show him I could be into music like him. He would dismiss my attempts and use that as an opportunity to throw another one of my golden siblings achievements in my face.

I started drawing at 9 and I was so excited about the reaction from my teachers, classmates and family well everyone except him. My older brother was also an artist so of course my drawings couldn't compare to his even though he was 17 years older than I was! I kept drawing though but I found myself criticizing my work just like he was it was never good enough despite what everyone else thought. I convinced myself I was just being a perfectionist but the reality was with every picture I drew, with every stroke I painted on canvas I could hear his voice telling me it was not good. I went through so many art forms trying to find one that gave me that peace and joy but it was always short lived while he was in the back of my head.

Because of the years of division he caused between my siblings especially my sister I did not like them. Every time I was around them I felt inferior because of him. I spent years resenting them for getting the love I wanted from him . All of his friends and clients got to see this man I never knew they thought he was the greatest guy so nice, funny and a healer. I experienced his abuse in the home where he would break me down to tears every chance he got. It was always so confusing seeing him outside the home be nice and then just like a dark cloud was living over our home feel his darkness take over.

When I was about to turn 12 he decided his life was too short and he no longer wanted to stay married to my mom. I did not know how to feel like on one hand I was happy to not have to deal with everyday but I did not know what that would mean for me since I never lived in a home without him. After the divorce I went from seeing him everyday to every other weekend. You would think seeing him less would be better but not for me it was like getting a concentrated version of him and then spending two weeks to recover just in time to be tormented again. I hated visitation with him I could feel his heavy spirit linger when he dropped me off and I was so angry I started taking it out on my mom. I felt like I was becoming him as young as I was it was like he was transferring his evilness to me and I hated feeling that way. I bled on people that did not cut me and I would feel remorse but could not apologize. I started building a thick skin just to prepare to see him and for the next 3 years I was on a constant emotional rollercoaster. When I was 15 my mom gave me the option to stop going on these visits seeing how much of an emotional toll it was taking on me. I gladly took that opportunity to stop going.

I still spoke to him via text but he even found a way to make me feel bad through text. If I needed something and he was in a good mood he would give it to me and send all these nice emojis. If he was irritated and I reached out to him he would respond in all caps and tell me to ask my mom instead. I slowly just stopped communicating with him unless I absolutely had to and his texts started going ignored.

I kept drawing and started to feel more confident in my talents the more I was away from him. My plan was to become big one day and show him all of his abuse did not stop me from making my dreams come true. I wanted to show him that I was also golden like my siblings and I deserved that love too. I never got that chance because right before I turned 18 he died suddenly. I was so mad how could he die before I was able to prove him wrong. I wanted so bad to feel grief that he was gone but if I am completely honest I was mad. I still felt he had a hold on me and how far I could go even more so that he was gone. I could hear him criticizing me louder and I felt myself having anxiety about my future and not becoming anything.

My mom suggested I go through therapy and sort out those feelings and start my journey to healing. Those sessions did help but joining this group to share my story with people that have gone through it as well has really been the breakthrough I needed. Since I joined this group I became a full time graphic design artist and a published illustrator. Even though my dad was a nightmare I get to live out my dreams now that he is gone. I have never felt so free to be exactly who I was born to be a melanin rich, gifted and a talented artist.

Thank you so much for sharing Charity. In my time mentoring Charity we talked about her being the scapegoat child for her father. The scapegoat child is the child in the family has been trained to submit to the narcissistic parent early on learning their feelings do not come first they often times grow up to be people pleasers and overly critical of themselves. Narcissistic parents use their dominance over this child to feed their need for control. They become aware of the weaknesses of the scapegoat children and will use this to give everything the scapegoat child wants to the golden children to further torment the scapegoat child.

The feelings of passive aggressiveness after being in contact with her father is common in narcissistic parent/ child relationships. Narcissistic parents instill fear in the children and silence them into not being emotional in front of them by ridiculing and gaslighting them into submission. The child will then take out that rage on individuals they feel safe with which creates a toxic outlet for them where they will "bleed" on people who did not cut them in order to purge those feels they were forced to keep in.

All of the stories told so far the narcissist in their lives have been the same type of narcissist a malignant aggressive one. These narcissist are easier to spot due to outward displays of aggression, selfishness and are often more outgoing. Our last story is about Tracy's ex husband a covert vulnerable narcissist.

Psychologists have named the covert narcissist the most dangerous one. Covert narcissist are like helping a wounded wolf thinking you are helping a wounded dog. They appear helpless and just needing a little help from their supply however they are devious and constantly scheming to destroy their oblivious supply. Due to the quiet manipulation it can take the supply years to realize the abuse they are going through and how all of their efforts are being sabotaged behind the scenes. Covert narcissist still have the same selfish need for admiration and validation but suffer from self esteem issues and use their victimhood to conditioned those around them to give them their attention.

Tracy will now be sharing her journey through her marriage with Marcus. Please give her your attention and support.

A Stranger in My House

Thank you Margaret, hi everyone like she mentioned my name is Tracy. Growing up I was raised by a single mother who taught me to believe that there is a good in everyone and to give them the benefit of the doubt. Back then the word narcissist was not something we ever talked about or even knew what it was. My father was in my life but had a separate family that I would visit two weekends a month. While I was in his home I was known as the peacemaker between my siblings to avoid being punished. Early on I learned to read a room and could feel the emotions of those around me.

My father was an alcoholic and was not home a lot of the times I visited due to hanging out with friends or his other women. The times I did spend with him he was drunk but he was a friendly drunk so I took the quality time any way I could. My mother was the one who helped me with communication, compassion and having a firm foundation. When I was younger I did not see her in many relationships and the one my father was in was a toxic one so I waited until I was an adult to even try to be in a relationship.

Once I started dating I found myself being in relationships where the men were emotionally unavailable and intimidated by me. I am not an aggressive person but I am ambitious and once I have an idea I sprint toward it until I am done with it. In my quest for finding safety in relationships I would write out my vision and timeline that I would like to do things like be married and have children. Looking back it was naive of me to think I could plan a life with someone I did not have in my life without their input but like the saying goes if you want to make God laugh tell Him your plans.

My first serious relationship resulted in having my daughter but shortly after she was born we broke up. I had another serious relationship after that where I was briefly engaged but we were not on the same page on a lot of things so we did not last. After the second failed relationship I decided to focus on being a mother and went back to college to get my degree. I stayed single for 2 years and just as I was finishing my degree I joined a dating app to see what was out there.

I started writing my profile and I would put everything I was looking for so that if someone comes across it they would eliminate themselves if they did not meet my criteria. Like I said before I was naive and just gave the blueprint to all the men who want to pretend they are my perfect match. I saw Marcus' profile and his pics were decent seemed a little old and blurry but I hit the like on the profile. I set up my profile to send an auto message whenever I hit like so it was a personalized message instead of the template they created. When he got the message he sent me one back he asked me if it was his eyes that made me reach out. Confused I replied no but asked him about himself. He started telling me about himself saying he had a job, his own place and car. He said he worked with disabled adults. When I told him about my background and my belief in God he said that was great because he was a pastor.

He then asked me for my email address and we started communicating back and forth on there until we set up a date for a week later due to his work schedule. The more we talked the more I felt like I was talking to a male version of myself he was into the same things I was into but had been unlucky in love. He said as a child he suffered from a severe form of asthma that caused him to spend most of his childhood in the hospital. He said his ex wife was a cheater and was so terrible to him he lost his passion for basketball and art which he was a great artist according to himself. He told me he was extremely close with his family and they spent every Sunday having dinner and playing games. Although they never told him they were proud of him he said they were the reason he decided to become a pastor and they were all in the church that they had in his uncle's home every Sunday.

When we finally spoke on the phone he let me do most of the talking and said he was like an onion it took him time to open up. I thought that was a little weird but I also knew it takes time for some people getting comfortable opening up. When it came time for our first date we were both running late but I made it to the restaurant first and had to wait almost 40 minutes for him to show up. After all the conversations I was still excited to meet him even though I was annoyed at how late he was. When he finally showed up I gave him a hug and instead of apologizing for being late he blamed it on his brother who was having car trouble. In our previous conversations he told me he was allergic to mushrooms so when he went to order his meal without telling them to leave out the mushrooms I let the waiter know. I thought it was weird since this was his favorite restaurant he did not let them know that but shrugged it off. While sitting there he acted like he was shy and would barely look at me while we were talking. He did not seem like the confident person he portrayed himself to be online but maybe he was just nervous I thought.

At the end of dinner a lady said we looked like a cute couple and asked if she could take a picture of us which we let her know it was just our first date. I felt like this was a sign we were a good match. When he walked me to the car and we talked for a little bit then he gave me a hug and walked to his car. He was such a gentleman I thought most guys would try to kiss you but he just gave me a hug. After that date the love bombing began we had the next date a few days later at his family's house for Sunday dinner and his family loved me and his brother told me how much Marcus liked me and he hoped we would be together. We had fun going on date after date and on the 5th date he finally kissed me and on my way home he sent me a text asking if I would be his girlfriend. I told him I would and the next date he told me that he loved me and he knows I am who God wants him to be with. Everything was moving so fast but I thought maybe this again was a sign we were supposed to be together.

When he met my daughter she hung on to him as if she knew him already and as he was leaving she told him she loved him. It seemed he was passing all the tests from the people in my life and even strangers. When we would go to his family gatherings in the beginning he was always laughing and joking with them and they seemed like the tight knit family he told me he had. That started to change the more involved we got. It was like his family was trying to warn me about his character by telling me stories of his selfishness and how he never bought them any gifts but expected them to give him grand gifts. They would also tell me how he never called them unless he needed money or something from them. I remember one day when we were leaving their house he went into a rage about how badly they talked about him and how they treated him like he was still a child and how that was the old him. I tried to calm him down but after that I started seeing that group of family only briefly on holidays.

We almost broke up due to him continuously showing up late when we were supposed to go on dates. He came so late one time the restaurant was about to close when he casually showed up to my house. I was livid I told him he needs to respect my time and if he tells me he is going to be there at a certain time that he should honor his word. I was so upset I started crying and he just stared at me blankly until I stopped. He then said he did not know what to say but he heard me. After that he never gave me a specific time just a range which he always came in the later part of it.

He worked night shifts and I worked days so the times we spent together were mostly date nights until he switched his day off to mines. When we started to spend our day off together I noticed the dates started becoming less and he would just come over to wash his clothes, eat and sleep until he went to work the following day. As my lease was ending we decided to move into together. After moving in together he was still working nights and overtime so when he was not working nights he still stayed up all night. At first I did not mind because I was working days and sleep but I noticed while he was up he was always playing videos games and on his phone so I asked him why. He told me he had a brother that died and right before he died they bonded over playing video games and playing now helped him cope and feel closer to him. He said he had a strained relationship with his older brother and always wanted to be like him so he would steal his clothes to get any type of attention from him even if it meant negative attention. I was close to my siblings so I felt bad he did not have a good relationship with his so I found myself being conditioned to letting him have his way by playing video games anytime he wanted and not making it an issue. He made light of it saying at least I knew he was not out in the streets.

Moving into together we never sat down to discuss how we would split up the bills and because my daughter was also living with us I felt obligated to buy groceries for the house. Buying groceries turned into paying all the utilities on top of my half of the rent. He would tell me stories about his ex-wife and how she never worked and he had to pay for everything having multiple jobs to take care of them. I have always been independent so I felt like I had to prove I was not like that and fell right into his trap of taking on the bulk of the financial responsibilities. He spent money frivolously even in the beginning anytime he had extra money it would go to a new phone or latest video game. He was always talking how being a father was so important to him and how much he loved my daughter like his own but when it came to financially support her he always found a new expense that tied up his money. We opened a joint account so that I could put him on my health insurance since he needed asthma medicine and did not have a job that had benefits. I was the only one who put money into it and always found a reason to withdraw it.

After two years of being together we started discussing marriage and having a child together. At this time his job had stopped giving him overtime but instead of looking for another job he just started going to play basketball in his free time and playing more video games. I got promoted at my job so I had more money coming in and started to buy more things for my daughter and for the house. He started noticing this and all of sudden he was depressed because he could not get a promotion on his job. He asked me to help him look for another job so we could get married. Well me thinking that maybe if he made more he would actually contribute hopped at the chance to make life a little easier. The more I applied the more I saw him playing the game and always on his phone. I would ask if he got any call backs and he would say no and one day I just stopped asking. I slowly stopped applying and figured he would get to it if he really wanted it. As we approached our third year together he said he was looking for rings for me and showed me a magazine to see the type I liked. He then told me when he got it but said he wanted it to be a surprise of when he popped the question. Months went by and we were going to go out for his birthday and invited some friends and his family to dinner. I could feel that he was going to propose so I went and got my makeup and nails done in preparation hoping to look really nice. When we got to dinner he was nervous at first but as a soon the waiter took our order that nervousness became irritation. I noticed it and asked him what's wrong? 'You didn't see that waiter? He was only looking at you and was flirting with you!" I was so confused I had no idea what he was talking about. Every time the waiter came he would get more and more angry. His brother tried to talk to him knowing what his plans were for the night. He finally started to calm down which I was happy about I had never seen him like that before and did not like it. He stood up to give a speech that ended in him proposing to me. I said yes and after that emotional dinner I was glad it ended in the proposal I expected.

As we started to talk about our wedding plans he expressed wanting an actual wedding because his first one was thrown together and his family did not show up for him. I did not really want a wedding but gave in so he could have the wedding he wanted. We did not discuss a budget and he made sure to let me know he was not getting overtime at his job still. The wedding day was quickly approaching and he was still not helping with the costs but came with his plans on what he wanted along with a sad story on how he never got what he wanted in life. Although I was not making a lot I worked with my mom to give him the wedding he dreamed of. As the day became closer the less I saw him until our counseling session as we drove to the session he was eerily quiet not even playing music which was unlike him. We walked to the door of the pastor and he sheepishly knocked on the door. I was so confused because at the time I could not recall anything significant happening but decided to proceed to the session. We sat down and the pastor looked at Marcus for him to start talking so I directed my eyes in his direction. He started to stutter and told me, "Uh so uh I have something I need to tell you…" he said barely looking at me. Still confused as to what was going on I nod and he continues to tell me that a woman who I had never heard of was planning to crash our wedding! Stunned I asked him what he was talking about. He then tells me he was talking to her online and she confused what he said to her as him trying to be with her and when she found out he was getting married got upset and said she was going to stop it.

The pastor tried to intervene but I was so confused like was this man telling me he was not only cheating on me but the woman was planning to crash the wedding I paid for?!? In that moment I felt like I was in a nightmare what universe was I living in that I was planning a wedding while he was talking to other women? When you are hit with that type of news at least for me you do not ask the right questions and of course he knew I was not going to cuss his ass out in front of a pastor in hindsight that was pretty clever. I struggled to really focus on the rest of the session this had thrown me for a loop but one thing I do remember that pastor saying is, "what you accept before the altar is what you accept after the altar." It was not until after we were heading toward divorce did I connect the dots. The pastor was letting me know that Marcus was cheating on me and if I married him that was not going to stop and he was right.

We did get married and I can say with a clear conscience it was one of the worst days of my life it was a sign I ignored. The night ended with him crying on the floor that his family had not shown up for him and me consoling him while he told me he had to go back to work early so we would not get a honeymoon. Our honeymoon and marriage was over before it began I just did not know it.

Being married to Marcus was like being the wife, husband, mother and father. I worked while he slept and I planned while he spent his money how he wanted. After our child was born it got even worse he stayed away for hours saying he was at the gym but in reality he was spending time with other women he met online. Every time I tried to bring up his responsibilities to our family he would have an excuse and say he was depressed and knew I deserved more but he did not know how. I suggested he speak with his siblings who were married and taking care of their families but he would say he was embarrassed he was not taught like them and did not know how to ask. He was very good at making me feel sorry for him but that sympathy quickly turned into resentment. What was the point of being married when I still felt single. I was literally raising a defiant grown ass man who took zero accountability but wanted all the benefits of married life but none of the responsibility. I was no longer attracted to the version of the man I met because I could see that was not the man I married. One day we woke up and his car was repossessed he never even mentioned he was behind for months because I was giving him extra money to pay it. When I questioned him on where the money had gone he said on other bills. I think that was my last straw because I felt something in me change that day I pulled away and started living a separate life with myself and my children. I made sure the household was financially stable but I kept money for myself and my children. It became clear I had to put myself first because Marcus made sure he did. We went on for years on opposite schedules and separate lives we would come together for his family or friends events so he could keep up appearances like we were the perfect couple then he would leave in a separate car and stay gone for hours. I went to my family events alone with the kids so much my family thought Marcus was imaginary and when he did show up it would be late grab a plate and go.

I was in a state of apathy going through the motions until one night I started to feel the loneliness. I decided to pray that night and I asked God, "God please remove anyone and anything thing that is no longer serving me." I felt a sense of relief but had no idea of all the things and people in my life that were going to be removed and revealed. We had started traveling as a couple after that and every trip was constant arguing I realized for years I never really saw him in the light of day so days spent with just him I could see clearly how much of a miserable, negative person he was and was sick of his constant complaining. Although we were together for years he never knew who I was as much as I did not know who he was so trying to come together for these trips showed me who I was with, a stranger. On one of the trips I received a message from our landlord that they were planning to sell the home we rented. I stared at the message and my mind went to my prayer that house was being removed from my life. I tried to ask

Marcus what he wanted to do but as usual he bounced it back to me to make the decision for us. I decided to move to another state that would be better to raise our kids in and he agreed to the move since he had no other alternative plan for us.

For weeks I started planning the move and he was gone more and more saying he had to get multiple jobs to help pay for the move. Now in all the time we had been together he had never had an urgency to help us financially that fell on me so it was odd but it gave him the freedom he wanted to be away from the house while I did all the work. I was so busy figuring things out I barely noticed him missing from the house until the kids told me they missed him and had not seen him in awhile. When I confronted him about it he stopped me and said, "You deserve to be happy and I am not the man to do it." I stopped talking and let the words sink in I remember taking a few steps back stunned, "was this really happening?" It was I felt the tears well up in my eyes I still said nothing but I knew it was God releasing me. For a moment I had forgot Marcus was still in the room until he slumped on the bed and said, "I guess that's how you must've been feeling all a long huh?" I know this man is not trying to turn this around like I was the one who just broke up with him?!? Of course he is that is what he does but I did not take the bait I let my tears fall as he then said, "I am not moving with you and the kids you all are going to move and I am staying here I will visit you but I am not moving." He said it so plainly no other explanation was given I left the room and went out with my girls to cheers to my divorce. I felt a sense of relief I was finally going to be free from the years of running on the hamster wheel and going no where.

I foolishly thought that since he was the one to discard me that I would have a clean break from him. How wrong I was leading up to my move he tried to back track his statements but it was too late I was completely done my prayers had been answered. He started getting his allies together with his story on how he lost his family and just wants another chance. He gave his smear campaign to anyone who would listen anyone who had not seen the real him. I heard him talking one day to an in law and at first I was just going to ignore it since I was still planning for my move but decided no I was going to tell the truth. I spent hours on the phone exposing him for the real narcissist he was they were stunned because they like all of his family and friends thought we were the perfect couple. Knowing little at that time about the lengths a narcissist will go to keep up the facade I had no idea the price he was going to try and make me pay for exposing him but at that time I was just over it all.

Once I left he did everything he could to make us feel his absence he started to try and manipulate the kids as if he was not the one to leave them. He tried to use our youngest against our oldest by making him the golden child he would call him but not our oldest so much that our youngest asked him why. He tried to use his money to try to hurt us by not giving me anything to help with the kids and when I would ask he would take me through hoops until I stopped asking. As we were going through the divorce he would not comply with the court orders and would constantly change what he wanted in the divorce so that it would appear we could not agree. The problem with trying to impact someone is you would have had to have already had an impact on them to begin with. Because he was so absent throughout our marriage the kids had already gotten used to him not being around so him not living with us actually caused them to thrive even more in their environment. He had spent years not helping with our finances or contributing so even though I could have used the money I was used to having to figure it out. When it came to the divorce it was frustrating how long it took to finalize everything but without him in our lives I was and still am the happiest I have ever been. I finally was able to focus on being myself not in survival mode with all the resentment watching him do nothing while I did everything. I was able to be there for my kids even more and I saw them blossom everyday and because I was happy they were too. I was able to find love real love after divorcing him because fortunately I did not lose myself completely being with him I spent years being alone while married so I knew who I wanted to be and the love I really deserved which came to me once I was free. I am now remarried to someone who makes me feel safe to be myself and takes care of not only me but my kids as well. Today I am so happy to tell my story to people who understand but now that I have done that I am looking forward to putting it behind me and live my best authentic life. Thank you for letting me share.

"Thank you for sharing your story with us Tracy." Margaret said. I understand how empowering it can be to tell your truth when you have been conditioned to stay silent throughout the abuse. Covert narcissists use their victim story to get the things they want in life unlike an overt narcissist that use their aggressive behavior. Because the covert narcissist lacks self esteem they learn early on how to use their sad stories and circumstances on compassionate people in hopes they can manipulate them into getting whatever they want.

However when it comes to maintaining what they asked for they will blame the world for not teaching them how when they lose it. As Tracy mentioned the constant cheating in her marriage the narcissist is always in need of a new supply no matter what they have at home they need someone to validate them and how they want to be perceived in the world so they will find someone or something to do that at all times. If they cannot get it easily they do not want it that goes for admiration, material things and all forms of love. Being with a covert narcissist can feel like a slow burn that by the time it is in a full blaze you are amazed at how long you were in it and did not see what they were doing. In Tracy's situation Marcus used his work schedule to hide in plain sight while Tracy did all the work he sat back and let her so he could do what he wanted.

I am so proud that even though we may not have ended things before it happened we survived some of the worst people in the world and lived to tell our stories. Well this is the end of this session I am looking forward to hearing more as we have more individuals that have come forward and ready to share their experiences.

End of the Road

Our marriage was like riding on a two person bicycle with me in the front and you behind me you started off peddling in the very beginning but then you put your feet up and let me peddle for the rest of the way. You kept cheering me on like it was both of us in it but in reality it was just me peddling uphill downhill sweating making sure that we were getting to our destination. You kept cheering me on "you got this you got this" while your feet were kicked up and you were just enjoying the ride. When I got burned out you still just let me keep peddling along while you sit back and enjoyed the ride.

While adding more responsibility and kids I still peddled alone while you made sure you had enough water for you but not us as I kept peddling. I would ask you where our destination was because I was burning out and you would tell me you trusted where I was going and I would figure it out while you kicked back and did enough pretending like you were peddling too. Now I'm ready to get off the bike because I finally realized it has just been me all along and you admitting it out loud was just confirmation that is where you are at and I need and deserve more.